GOLF
tips

GOLF
tips

The Complete Guide to Improving Your Game

ALLEN F. RICHARDSON

p

About the Author

Allen F. Richardson is the author of two previous books about sport, one of them being *The Encyclopedia of Golf Techniques* which he co-wrote with PGA pro Chris Meadows. He has also written for a wide variety of newspapers and magazines on both sides of the Atlantic, including *The New York Times*, *USA Today* – for which he was the London correspondent for 10 years – *Glamour* and *Life*. In addition, he has served as a consultant to television news and documentary teams in the USA, UK, and Germany.

This is a Parragon Publishing Book

First published in 2001

Parragon Publishing
Queen Street House
4 Queen Street
Bath BA1 1HE, UK

Copyright © Parragon 2001

Designed, produced, and packaged by
Stonecastle Graphics Limited

Designed by Paul Turner and Sue Pressley
Photography by Bill Johnston
Photographic supervision by Chris Meadows
Edited by Philip de Ste. Croix

ISBN 0-75256-593-1

Printed in China

CONTENTS

INTRODUCTION

GOLF CAN drive you mad! From the first moment a golfer picks up a club, he or she is confronted with a paradox absent from most other sport: the game is enjoyable to the point of addiction, while also frustrating and humbling. But that paradox is what keeps golfers coming back for more, once they have hit a few buckets at the range or played a few rounds. Whether they come to the game as natural athletes, or from the ranks of the hopelessly inept, most golfers will not be particularly good at the start. But most are certainly good enough to hit a few wondrous shots that remain fixed in the mind like a photograph, and leave one hungry for more.

Like love, golf is also seductive, and most golfers want to be better practitioners. Soon, they are taking lessons, buying instructional books and videos, and wandering the aisles of superstores and pro shops, delighting in row upon row of the shiny new toys that manufacturers pour onto the market on an almost daily basis.

That's where *Golf Tips* comes into play. With no apologies, this book is tailored to the needs of the vast majority of golfers who want to improve their games, but don't have all the time in the world to do so. The pages inside are compact and the instruction concise, though the knowledge imparted is bountiful and the illustrations numerous. Instead of cutting to the bone, *Golf Tips* goes straight to the marrow.

Why 18 Holes?
Golf clubs once had a variety of holes, with St. Andrews possessing 12. The first 11 went out to the end of a peninsula. The golfers then came in by playing the first ten greens again, and finishing on a solitary green by the clubhouse, for a round of 22. But in 1764, the club decided to convert the first four into two, so the round went from 22 to 18. Other clubs soon followed suit.

Below: Mastering the fundamentals of the swing helps lower scores and makes golf more fun.

Several sections deal with how to choose the right equipment and the fundamentals of the basic swing, which is the key to learning how to hit consistently good shots. But after that, the emphasis of this book is different from some. *Golf Tips* focuses on real problems faced by real golfers, and concentrates on ways of cutting your score that do not assume the physical ability of a Lee Westwood, Sergio Garcia, or Tiger Woods.

Several sections deal with the short game, practice, course strategy, rules and etiquette, how to get out of trouble, how to cure common faults, how to cope with the constantly changing weather – and, finally, a section on advanced shotmaking, so you can take your game to the next level.

Along the way, *Golf Tips* also debunks a few myths that most golfers have heard from parents, friends, or fellow golfers who should know better. At the same time, this book fights the tendency of many golfers to over-analyze their games, and become too mechanical. After all, golf *is* just a game in the final analysis, and once the fundamentals are mastered, the object is to go out and play – trusting the swing you have developed – and to have some fun.

Of course, golf will still drive you mad. But after reading *Golf Tips*, hopefully you will not be grooving idiosyncrasies or bad habits into your swing, you'll be scoring much better, and you will enjoy the best moment of all, gathering with family and/or friends after a round to relive the preceding hours, and then to prepare for the next golf outing.

Above: Improving your short game and sinking a few more putts per round will also dramatically lower your scores and provide some tales to tell back at the clubhouse.

CHOOSING THE RIGHT CLUBS

BUYING GOLF clubs has become almost as complicated as choosing a new computer. With dozens of manufacturers clamoring for the golfer's attention and a constant stream of new products flooding the market, even the most experienced golfers can be confused. The variety of outlets is also growing, with clubs sold everywhere from the high street to online.

But in recent years, a choice that was once open to only a select few – the purchase of clubs specifically designed for one's physique and talent level – is now available to an increasing number of golfers. Custom-fitted clubs are often the way to go. Many superstores and specialty golf shops have compact driving ranges where you can try a variety of clubs, and computers to analyze your swing.

> **Great Golf Tip:**
> • Stronger, more athletic women and juniors might be better suited to using men's clubs rather than those specifically designated for them.

Opposite: Many golfing outlets now have interchangeable components that allow you to try a number of shafts, grips, and lie angles.

Below: Pro shops can make you feel like a kid in a candy store. But try to focus on what's essential to your game, and resist the rest.

But if you are already taking lessons from a qualified PGA pro, you can ask him or her to lend you demonstration clubs, and suggest a line that fits your body type, swing, and even sense of style. Owning a customized set of clubs is like treating yourself to a tailored suit of clothes. You will almost inevitably gain confidence and improve your game. Generally, the price will not hurt that much either, with several manufacturers increasingly vying for this market.

If you do shop for yourself, keep in mind some basic facts about clubs: the swingweight, lie angle, type of shaft, and thickness of the grips. Swingweight is an individual choice, so actually swinging the club is the only way to determine what suits you. Lie angle must conform to your build, and if it does not, you will hit shots off to the left or right. Shafts are made of steel or various new space-age compounds. They also come in different degrees of flex and length. Determining the right shaft depends on your skill, strength, physique, and individual preference. Finally, consider grip size. If the grips are too thick, you might slice, while thin grips can encourage a hook.

Beginners and younger players might also opt for a half set, which often contains the odd-numbered irons, a few woods, a wedge, and a putter. Half sets are especially suited to kids, since they grow out of most things quickly, but can help any golfer focus better when they play. Using fewer clubs tests versatility and imagination on the course.

Great Golf Tips:

• Consider perimeter-weighted clubs, versus more traditional bladed clubs. With a cavity back and oversized clubhead, these modern irons are more forgiving because of a larger sweet spot.

• As you age, try more flexible shafts to aid clubhead speed. If you are tall, use longer shafts to take tension off the back.

• Follow your instinct when choosing a putter. What feels right is probably best suited to your game.

GOLF BALLS AND CLOTHING

A BEWILDERING ARRAY of choices awaits the golfer when selecting the right ball for his or her game. That's the bad news. The good news is that with so much choice, you can now purchase exactly the right ball for your game. With increased competition, prices are also lower.

Golf balls are generally divided into two types, according to the way they are constructed, designated as either two-piece or three-piece balls. Most golfers opt for the two-piece ball, which usually has a cover made of *surlyn* – a tough, durable plastic – and an inside filled with various compounds designed to make the ball fly farther.

Low handicappers and pros often use a three-piece ball, which has a cover usually made of *balata*, a soft, easily cut rubber compound that gives the ball more feel and spin, but that sacrifices some distance and durability. Inside the ball is

Below: Soft spikes are rapidly replacing metal ones. If you buy shoes with metal spikes, make sure they are changeable, and carry a set of plastic spikes in your bag.

Left: A good golf glove is essential, but the proper fit is even more important. Insist on trying a glove on before purchase.

a liquid center and a layer of wound fabrics. The three-piece ball is often more expensive than the two-piece.

Recently, manufacturers have attempted to combine the attributes of both types of golf ball by introducing a urethane cover, which is durable *and* soft.

The choice of golf apparel used to be governed by the rules of local clubs, and a handful of garment manufacturers, which narrowed down choices. But now, with major designers weighing in, as golf becomes more 'fashionable,' the selection is almost endless. The real key, however, should be comfort and adaptability to the changing weather. Modern space-age fabrics have made that simple. You can now look good, and feel comfortable, when playing golf in almost any climate.

Different styles of golf shoes are also multiplying like mushrooms after a rain, but the key is to select a shoe that fits both your feet and the conditions you play in. Take into consideration the local rules where you will play as well. Many courses are now moving toward banning metal spikes, and demanding that you switch to soft, plastic ones.

Great Golf Tips:

• Buy different golf balls for different courses. A harder golf ball plays well on long courses with large greens. A softer ball with more spin is better suited to short courses and small greens.

• Choose golf clothing with modern fabrics that breathe in the heat, or shut out the wind. Clothing should also 'give' in the right places, so you will not restrict your swing.

• If you often play in the rain, buy golf shoes that can withstand a good soaking and keep your feet dry. However, if you play more often on hard, dry ground, select shoes that are lighter and have leather soles that can breathe.

THE PERFECT GRIP

THE FOUNDATION of a good golf swing starts with the set-up, which is composed of certain fundamentals that must be mastered first by anyone who hopes to improve their game. These include a solid grip, the proper alignment, and a good posture when addressing the ball.

A good grip is a thing of beauty, as the legendary Ben Hogan once said, though few golfers spend enough time learning a proper grip. But consider that the hands are the only part of the body that come into contact with the club, and that through the grip you impart power and shape your shots. Consider also that any number of swing faults are the result of poor grips.

Most golfers now use the Vardon grip, which was popularized by the early British great, Harry Vardon. This grip blends the hands so that they work together in the swing, and one does not dominate the other.

Great Golf Tips:
• The proper grip aids the set-up. With the right hand lower on the shaft, the left shoulder automatically sets slightly higher than the right, and the head is behind the ball.
• Learning a proper grip can take months. Assume your grip as often as possible and get used to it without hitting golf balls. If possible, grip a club while watching television or working.

Below: Grips can be highly individualistic, but there are three basic types, starting with the interlocking (left), which is ideal for golfers with small hands, followed by the Vardon (center) and baseball (right), which is used mostly by beginners and children.

Here's how to assume the Vardon grip

• Let your hands hang naturally by your sides, then rest the club in your left hand, leaving a half-inch protruding at the top. Position the club so it runs from the middle joint of the forefinger to the bottom joint of the little finger. Finally, wrap the fingers around, laying the club against the fleshy pad at the bottom of the hand. The thumb should fall slightly to the right of center down the shaft.

• Add the right hand by first putting the little finger in the cleft between your left forefinger and middle finger, then wrapping the rest of the fingers around the club, laying the crease in your palm over the thumb of the left hand. Complete the grip by laying your right thumb diagonally across the top, with the tip resting lightly against the forefinger.

Below: Mastering a solid grip will also help to set up the proper body angles, with the right shoulder slightly lower than the left, and the head behind the ball.

In a correct grip, you should see at least two and a half knuckles on the left hand. This is a 'strong' grip, and will return the clubhead square to the ball, preventing the most common fault of most golfers – a slice. The 'V's' formed between the thumb and forefinger of both hands should point toward your right shoulder.

Great Golf Tip:
• Most golfers grip too tightly, which can wreck the best swing. Hold the club as lightly as possible, though firmly enough to control it so your hands do not come off during the swing.

ALIGNMENT AND POSTURE

THE REMAINING elements of the set-up include alignment and posture. We take a proper stance by placing, or aligning, the body at correct angles to the ball and target line. The key word here is parallel. In golf, you line up the feet, hips, and shoulders along an imaginary line to the target, with your body parallel to that line and the feet roughly shoulder- width apart.

Body weight should be evenly distributed between both feet, which should be comfortably angled out about 10 to 20 degrees. Such a stance promotes a strong, balanced position.

Posture is the final ingredient. Assume a dynamic posture over the ball by first standing straight and tall, then bending forward from the hips. As you do this, your rear should jut out slightly and your back should stay straight. Lastly, flex your knees, allowing your weight to settle over the back half of your feet.

Great Golf Tips:
• Practice alignment by placing a club along the target line, then another to the right of that and parallel to the first. Place a third to the left and parallel to the other two, then take away the target-line club. Line the feet, hips, and shoulders up with the nearest club and hit balls from between the two clubs.
• Check posture and alignment in a mirror, or on video, making sure the back is not rounded.

Right: The ideal set-up promotes a smooth, powerful swing.

Below: Position the ball off the left instep or heel for the driver, moving back to the center for the short irons and wedges.

Spine Angle/Swing Plane

AN EXCELLENT set-up provides the foundation for an equally good swing. But when the time comes finally to swing a club in anger, a golfer needs to focus on two other keys: the ability to maintain a consistent spine angle and to stay within what is called the swing plane.

Imagine the spine angle as a straight line drawn down your back. During the swing, you will want to maintain that angle, turning around this line as if it were an axis.

Now imagine a pane of glass that extends from your shoulders to the ball, with your head poking through a hole at the top. When you turn in the swing, your shoulders should stay within the glass pane, or perpendicular to your spine angle. This is your swing plane, and the route your club takes is called the swingpath. Any major deviation will produce any number of bad shots.

> **Great Golf Tips:**
> • As with posture, the only way to check your spine angle or swing plane properly is by practicing in front of a mirror. Taking a lesson, or having a friend watch is also helpful.
> • Check swing plane in a mirror as well. Swing a short iron to the top. An imaginary line extending from the butt end of the grip to where the ball is should fall directly across the right shoulder.

Below: Good posture leads directly to maintaining spine angle and a correct swing plane.

THE PRE-SHOT ROUTINE

CONSISTENCY IS an absolute must in golf. In order to score well, a golfer must routinely hit good shots, and the key to establishing such consistency starts with a pre-shot routine. Approach each shot in the same way, developing a routine to lay the framework for success.

Start the pre-shot routine by standing behind the ball and visualizing the shot you want to hit. Scrutinize the golf hole, select a target, and calculate the distance. Factor in how the ball is likely to fly and how far it will roll once it hits the ground. Finally, conjure an image of the shot in your mind, from the time it leaves the clubhead until it lands.

Below: The pre-shot routine starts with picking out a target, then placing the clubhead at a right-angle to the target line. Finally, line up your feet, hips, and shoulders parallel to the target line.

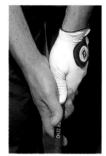

Next, imagine a line from the ball to where you want it to go, then pick an intermediate target a few inches in front of the ball. This might be a blade of grass or a twig. When you take your stance, you can use this intermediate target to line up correctly to the ball, since it is easier to visualize the target line by using something nearby, rather than far away.

Now it is time to address the ball. Take the club in the right hand and move from behind the ball to the left side. Place the clubhead on the ground behind the ball – using the intermediate target to line up – then position your feet, hips, and shoulders parallel to the imagined target line. Finally, add your grip, swivel your head and focus on the real target for a split second, freezing the image in your mind. This last bit of advice will keep you from obsessing about your golf swing.

But, at this point, many golfers freeze up, and tension is the enemy of all golf shots. The antidote is called the waggle. Take a deep breath, flex your fingers, waggle the clubhead lightly, and try to drain away any tension that might have crept into your hands, arms, or shoulders. Some golfers take a miniature backswing when they waggle, while others just wave the clubhead around the ball. Figure out what works best for you and stick with it.

Above: Tension usually starts in the hands, but can invade the whole body and destroy your swing motion. Waggle the club to drain tension away and rehearse your swing.

Great Golf Tips:
• The pre-shot routine is a mini-rehearsal for hitting the ball. Watch the pros. They have a routine that rarely varies.
• Take a practice swing before you start the pre-shot routine, and do it well away from the teeing area and/or the ball.
• When visualizing a shot, take into consideration the lie of the land, noting especially any trouble that you may encounter, such as a sand trap, trees, or water. Then line up on the side of the tee where the hazard is and aim in the opposite direction.

THE BACKSWING

A T THE start of the swing, the golfer moves the clubhead away from the ball to a pre-determined position at the top, depending on how far he or she wants to hit the ball. If done correctly, this move can set up a chain of events that result in an excellent strike, propelling the ball in an accurate and powerful flight toward the target. But if this move is faulty, the opposite effect takes over, leading to any number of mistakes.

Start the backswing by taking the club away from the ball in a low, slow arc, keeping the triangle formed by your hands, arms, and shoulders in unison with the upper torso. This is known as the 'connected swing,' and means that the golfer is

Great Golf Tip:
• Wrap your right hand around the lower part of your left forearm, then swing back. You will find yourself in the correct position at the top, and that your weight has shifted over to your right side automatically. Use this drill to ingrain the idea of a connected and stable backswing.

Below: Choke down on a club, placing the butt end against your chest. Swing back to waist high to feel the connected swing.

effectively using the large muscles of his or her upper body, rather than simply the hands and arms, to turn back from the ball.

In order to do this, however, you must *turn* your shoulders, rather than tilt them toward the ground. Many golfers tilt in an unconscious effort to stay connected with the ball, which results in leaving too much weight on the left side. That robs the swing of power and control. So let the upper torso dictate your movement, and as you do, your arms and shoulders will raise the club in a wide arc. At the same time, the right arm will fold slightly, the weight will move back over the right foot, and the hips will be pulled around to the right. Ultimately, your back ends up facing the target.

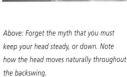

Above: Forget the myth that you must keep your head steady, or down. Note how the head moves naturally throughout the backswing.

Now you have come to a position with the club held on a line three-quarters or parallel to the ground – the wrists having bent naturally as the swing progressed – and your body coiled over the ball. What is meant by coil? As your body turns back, your legs and hips also turn, but not as far. This will happen naturally if you keep your left foot planted on the ground, or with most of it still in contact with the turf.

If you are truly athletic, you might also try to keep your hips from turning as much as you can, which will build more power into the swing by creating tension, or torque, as the lower body resists the turn of the upper body. But a word of warning. Trying to hold your hips back is an advanced move, and unless you are in superb shape, you will risk injury.

Great Golf Tips:

• Forget the old maxim about keeping the left arm 'straight' in the backswing. Most players will have some bend.

• One cliché remains a vital tip: a slight pause at the top will stabilize your swing and set up a correct downswing path.

• Never manipulate the hands or wrists, which should remain passive. They will cock naturally if you swing correctly.

• Do not let your chin droop. Keep it up to allow your left shoulder to swing freely underneath during the backswing.

THE DOWNSWING

A GOOD BACKSWING is only half the equation in taking a decent crack at the ball. How the golfer delivers the clubhead to the ball, and what he or she does after that, can spell the difference between a good and a bad shot. In other words, the downswing is more accurately referred to as the throughswing, because that is really what is happening. The golfer is swinging *through* the ball to a finish position.

But the natural tendency is often to rush things, throwing the club at the ball with the hands and arms, rather than again letting the body dictate the swing. Bobby Jones often said he liked to start down in leisurely way, which is a good swing key. Focusing on that idea will allow the body to uncoil in a reverse image of the backswing, starting from the ground up as the legs, hips, and upper torso move back toward the ball, and the weight shifts back to the left side. The arms and shoulders then follow naturally, delivering the clubhead to the ball.

What happens at impact? If you started with the correct fundamentals of the set-up – a good grip, stance, and posture – then executed a wide, flowing backswing, that was followed by an unhurried, gradual uncoiling into the throughswing: the answer is nothing. Nothing in the sense

Below: Practice the correct body movement without a club. In the throughswing, the left hip turns, or clears, through impact, while the right hand follows, swinging toward the target.

you need to worry about. The arms will straighten naturally, the hips will be angled to the left, the weight will shift forward, and the clubhead will meet the ball squarely.

The key point to remember about the impact position is that it is just part of the throughswing, not the be all and end all. In other words, carry on. Simply allow the ball to get in the way of a good swing. Let the body and the momentum built up by uncoiling the swing take you to a full, finished follow-through position. If you slow down, or quit on the ball, you will destroy the swing.

The finished position can tell you a lot about your swing. If you cannot hold the position, your swing was probably not connected and you did not shift your weight properly. The failure to finish in a balanced position means your swing also lacked balance.

Try to visualize a good finish at set-up, or through the swing itself, and this should help you to execute a better swing overall.

Above: Practice a baseball swing to gain a feel for weight shift and how the body turns away from the ball, then through the ball.

Great Golf Tips:

• Avoid trying to *hit* the ball. The ball should only get in the way of a good swing, rather than be the focus of your swing.

• Think of a photo finish! After completing your follow-through, try to hold that position for at least a few seconds.

• Swing a club upside down. The swoosh at the bottom proves that manipulating your hands at impact is not necessary.

THE COMPLETE SWING

BLENDING THE elements of a good backswing and downswing will eventually lead to an excellent movement that produces consistent shotmaking. At that point, these two seemingly separate elements are combined into a winning formula and become one: the complete swing.

Perhaps the best way to put a complete swing together is to do the opposite of what most golfers would think. Do not go to the driving range. Instead, stay home and swing a club over and over again, without a golf ball in sight. Study your alignment and posture in a mirror. Close your eyes and

Opposite: A variation on the pivot drill is to place a club behind your shoulders and concentrate on the correct way to turn. This is also a great way to loosen up before you begin a round.

Below: Learning the right mechanics is fine, but you must also have a feel for the swing. Close your eyes or swing blindfolded to develop this sense.

Great Golf Tips:

• Practice your swing with both feet close together. This drill promotes the proper weight shift, plus rhythm and tempo.

• Feel the clubhead. This will relax the hands and arms, slow the swing, and impart a sense of the correct swingpath.

• Try David Leadbetter's pivot drill. Put your right hand on your left shoulder and your left hand on your right shoulder, then turn back and forth. Doing this restricts extra movement, and ingrains the idea of coil and a proper weight shift.

practice the correct body turn, or grasp a basketball to your chest and work on keeping your arms and body connected in the swing, while shifting your weight properly. Watch some tapes of great golfers with fluid swings, trying to study those who most closely match your own height and frame.

But if you cannot resist a trip to the driving range, try to concentrate on rhythm and tempo. A smooth swing is one free of tension, so focus on draining any rigidity out of your grip, arms, and shoulders. Some golfers should also work on their back, hips, and even legs, which can become locked and restrict movement.

Try to slow down your swing as well. Most golfers swing too hard and fast, even when they think they are not. Whistling, humming a rhythmic tune, or counting 1, 2, 3 can help your timing. Swinging to a metronome is not a bad idea either, a practice aid that Payne Stewart often used.

THE BASIC PITCH SHOT

THE BASIC pitch shot is simply a miniature version of the full swing. But mastering this technique – which often calls for both feel and finesse – can dramatically lower your scores.

Working on the pitch – along with the rest of the short game – should be the cornerstone of your approach to golf. In any given round, shots from 60 yards (55m) in will account for over half your strokes, no matter how good your basic swing technique. Learning the short game – pitching, chipping, bunker play, and putting – is how you take a complete game from the driving range to the golf course.

Great Golf Tip:
• Devote some extra practice time to refining your pitch shot. Golfers who cannot hit the green in regulation on long par 4's can still save par with a good pitch. You will also increase your birdie chances on par 5's with a precise third shot into the green.

Below: Equalize the backswing and follow-through, hitting positively through the ball.

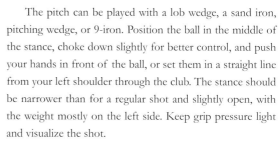

The pitch can be played with a lob wedge, a sand iron, pitching wedge, or 9-iron. Position the ball in the middle of the stance, choke down slightly for better control, and push your hands in front of the ball, or set them in a straight line from your left shoulder through the club. The stance should be narrower than for a regular shot and slightly open, with the weight mostly on the left side. Keep grip pressure light and visualize the shot.

A good pitch has a high trajectory and lands the ball softly with little roll. But that will not happen unless the shot is hit positively. Even though the pitch is a relatively delicate shot, failure to accelerate through the ball will result in a fat or thin hit. Be positive about how you play it and swing with an even rhythm and tempo.

How do you control distance? You can pitch from 60 yards (55m) to just off the green. Controlling how far the ball will travel is a matter of practice, and developing feel. Start at the range with a three-quarter swing, and try to keep both the backswing and follow-through even in length, working down to shorter swings at closer targets.

Gradually narrowing your stance can also restrict your turn, and shorten your swing naturally. You might try imagining your swing on a clock, with the three-quarter swing reaching 10 or 11 o'clock, then finishing at 1 or 2. Try swinging between 9 and 3 o'clock for shorter pitches of about 45 yards (41m). For pitch shots inside 35 yards (32m), keep your left wrist firm, though not rigid, through the follow-through.

THE BASIC CHIP SHOT

THE TECHNIQUE for hitting the basic chip shot is much like that for a putt. Keep that in mind and you will have a decided edge around the greens, where a good score can be made or broken. Use the chip to clear obstacles just in front of the ball – such as fringe grass, bare spots, or sandy, broken soil – and to get the ball running up to the flagstick.

How does the chip differ from a pitch? The pitch is hit high, the chip low. The pitch lands the ball softly, the chip makes it run. The pitch is played with a lofted club, the chip with either a wedge or anything down to a mid-range iron.

> **Great Golf Tip:**
> • As with any shot, assess your lie carefully. If the ball is sitting down in thick grass, open your stance and clubface, then factor in more roll.

Below: Keep your left wrist firm and your hands ahead of the clubhead.

> **Great Golf Tips:**
> • Try to land the ball on the green as soon as possible to ensure a truer roll. Focus on the landing area, not the hole.
> • Concentrate on rhythm and tempo, making sure you do not decelerate the club. Think about brushing the grass with your clubhead.
> • Read the green as you would for a putt. Once the ball lands, it will take the borrow in the same way a putt does.

Finally, a chip is generally played from about 35 yards (32m) in. Golfers sometimes mix up the two, and indecision can lead to poor shots.

Take a narrow stance, position the ball off the big toe of the right foot and keep the weight on the left side. Open the stance just slightly by pulling the left foot back from the target line, while keeping the hips and shoulders square. Grip the club low, almost down to the shaft, and set your hands in front of the ball.

When you visualize the chip, pick out the spot where you want to land the ball on the green. Use a smooth, unhurried stroke to strike the ball, mimicking the arms-and-shoulders pendulum motion of the putting stroke, while equalizing your backswing with the throughswing. Experiment with using either your regular grip, or a putting grip, to see which one is more comfortable and effective.

Only practice can tell you how to judge distance, and how to vary the length of your swing to produce the desired result. Practice from various distances around the green, and to various pin placements.

Try a variety of clubs as well. This is a shot that demands feel and imagination. Generally, the more lofted the club, the higher the ball will fly, and the shorter it will roll on the green. So if you are just off the putting surface, and the pin is close, use a sand iron or lob wedge. But if the pin is further away, use a longer iron and get the ball on the green as soon as possible, letting it roll most of the way to the pin.

Above: Try chipping with a 3- or 5-wood, which keeps the ball low and reduces the chance of an errant bounce.

BUNKER PLAY

INDING THE ball inside a sand trap often strikes fear into the heart of many golfers. But mastering the fundamentals of bunker play can reduce anxiety and save strokes, especially as the golfer comes to realize that this shot is really one of the easiest in the game.

Easy? As any pro will tell you, if he or she is going to hit a bad shot, landing in the sand is preferable to the rough. In a bunker the lie is usually better, and thus the shot more predictable. One can even impart spin to the ball and control where and how it lands.

The bunker shot is similar to a pitch, in that the club is swung out-to-in across the target line, with a smooth rhythm and tempo. Start by opening your stance, or aligning the feet, hips, and shoulders left of the target line. Then open the clubface *before* taking your grip, so the blade is square to the target. Finally, position the ball in the middle of the stance and focus on a spot one to two inches behind the ball. This is where the blade of the sand wedge shoulder enter the sand.

In bunker shots, the clubface never touches the

ball. Rather, the ball is lifted out on a sliver or cushion of sand. Some golfers call this an 'explosion shot.' But that implies the wrong approach. The bunker shot takes finesse and power, but the action is more akin to *splashing* the ball out.

Hover the club over the sand, then break your wrists early in the backswing, which should be slow and smooth. As with any shot, start the downswing with your body – not the hands and arms – slicing into the sand with a positive strike, and ending in a stable, finished position.

Above: During practice, draw lines to ingrain the idea of how to remove the sand and splash the ball out of the bunker.

Practice this shot from a variety of lies, learning how to adjust for distance and control by aiming at targets. Generally, the closer you are to the pin, and the higher the bunker face, the more you must open your stance and clubface, move the ball forward in your stance, and vary the length of your swing. The farther you are from the target, and the lower the lip, the less you open the stance and clubface, and the farther back you play the ball.

Finally, weaken your grip. Turning the hands to the left will avoid closing down the clubface and digging into the sand as you play the shot.

Below: Swing with a smooth, even tempo. Confidence is the key to hitting positive bunker shots.

PUTTING TECHNIQUE

HE OLDEST cliché in golf really does bear repetition: drive for show and putt for dough. Even the longest hitters can be humbled, and often by a less skillful player, when they reach the green. Putting can account for over half the strokes in a typical round, so mastering the putting stroke is vital to success in golf.

But what is the basic putting stroke? If you watch the pros, and especially the older ones on the senior tours in Europe and America, you will see almost as many putting techniques as golfers. Putting is highly individualistic. However, unless you are already playing scratch golf, you should aim to master the basic fundamentals of the modern approach to putting.

Most golfers now use the 'reverse overlap' grip, and try to swing the arms, hands, and shoulders in a uniform, pendulum-like stroke. Beyond that, the golfer needs feel and touch, the ability to judge distance, and the most vital ingredient of all when putting – confidence. Put some practice time into putting and confidence will follow.

The reverse overlap makes both hands work as a unit, keeps the wrists passive and naturally squares the putter blade. Here's how to assume the grip:

• Place your left hand on the putter, wrap the middle, third, and little finger around the grip, then point the thumb straight down.

• Put the fingers of your right hand on the club, with the little finger resting snugly against the middle finger of the left hand, and the right thumb also pointing straight down the putter grip.

Opposite: A ball dropped from your left eye should land directly onto the ball.

Below: The modern putting stroke using the reverse overlap grip and a back-and-forth pendulum motion.

• Finally, run the left forefinger straight down across the fingers of the right hand.

What about grip pressure? Tight hands will produce a jerky or incomplete motion. Try to grip the club lightly and evenly while you are putting.

Once you have mastered the proper grip, learning the right putting stroke is simple. Line up over the ball with your feet, hips, and shoulders square to the target line, and your dominant eye over the ball. Your hands should hang naturally in that position, forming an inverted triangle with your shoulders as the base, and the hands as the apex of the triangle.

Keep that triangle intact as you swing in a straight line back from the ball, then through it, equalizing the backswing and follow-through. The pendulum stroke allows you to move in a fluid and dynamic way, while concentrating on rhythm and tempo, as you stroke *through* the ball.

Great Golf Tips:

• Develop a consistent pre-shot routine for putting, and keep practice strokes to a minimum. Pick a target, line up the putter, then take your stance. Finally, swivel your head – rather than lifting it – to zero in on the target before taking your stroke.

• Never follow the putt with your eyes, as this will open the shoulders and send the ball offline. Stay focused on the spot your ball has just vacated for at least a few seconds.

• Take your glove off to aid feel and touch. This is also a subtle mental reminder that putting requires a different approach.

READING THE GREEN

LEARNING HOW to read a green is a true art, but it is easier than most golfers think. Start as soon as your approach shot lands. As you walk up the fairway, take in any visual clues offered, such as the contour of the land. Is water nearby? Is the green shaded or open to direct sunlight? Such factors can affect speed and the direction in which your putt will run.

Below: Crouch low to study the line of your putt and to judge the speed.

Once on the green, study the slopes within it and the direction of the grain of the grass. Walk around to get different perspectives, and, if possible, watch what happens when others putt. Finally, go to your ball and mark it, crouching behind to analyze what lies between you and the hole. If you have time, you might also walk to the hole and study that area more closely, while also looking back to gain a different view.

How do you sort all that out and hit the putt? Start with the *line*. Breaking putts – ones that bend due to the contour of the green – can drive even the best golfer crazy. The way to simplify this is to visualize a straight line to the hole. If you have a putt of 30 feet (9m), and you think the slope will make the ball bend three feet (1m) to the left or right, draw an imaginary line three feet to the side of the hole, and stroke your putt down that line.

The second major factor to consider is *speed*. If you hit your putt too hard down that

Left: Practice before a round to gain feel and confidence, lining up a few balls and listening to them drop into the hole.

Great Golf Tips:

• Practice with a piece of string secured to two stakes, placing one end where you will stand, and the other near the hole. Watch how the ball breaks off the line when it takes the borrow.

• The grain – the way stems of grass lie – provides vital clues as to speed. If shiny, you are putting with the grain and the ball will move quickly. If dull, you are putting against, and the ball will roll more slowly. Putting across the grain will make the ball bend in the direction of the grain.

• Overcome your fears and strike more aggressively on uphill putts, while shortening your motion for downhill ones. But on both, the key is to stroke positively through the ball.

• Short of holding up other golfers, you should take as long as you need to read the green and take your putt. Patience is always rewarded in putting.

imaginary line, it may well roll through the slope, or *borrow*, and thus past the hole. But if you hit it too slow, it might run out of steam and slide down the slope well short of the hole. Judging speed only comes with practice and experience, but the best way to assess this factor is by settling on the line first, then focusing on the speed.

Once you have read the line, take your set-up, using an intermediate target to align your putter blade. Then zero in on the hole, trying to feel how hard, or softly, you need to hit the ball to get it there. Take a practice stroke to help determine the pace, picture the area between you and the hole in your mind, and then hit your putt.

How to Practice

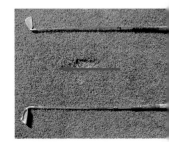

MOST GOLFERS waste their time on the practice range. They tend to hurry, often hit only the driver or long irons, and generally forget that golf is a game that not only demands length, but also accuracy, touch, and imagination. Practice with a purpose, and start by loosening up.

Spend the first few minutes doing basic exercises and pivot drills that will stretch and warm up the muscles, and thus prevent possible injury. Such activity also reminds you of the proper turn, coil, and weight shift in a good swing.

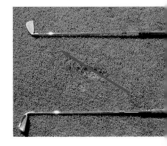

Next, focus on the fundamentals of a proper grip, alignment, ball position, and posture. Laying some clubs on the ground will help you to square up to the target line, place the ball in the right spot, and avoid practicing a fault that could turn into a habit.

Finally, pick up a short club and start swinging it, concentrating on establishing a smooth rhythm and tempo. Drain any tension from your hands, arms, shoulders, and back. Wiggle your toes to relax your feet and remind yourself that the swing is an athletic movement that starts from the ground up, and is built on a stable, yet dynamic, foundation.

Now you are ready to put a ball down. But before you do, vow that you will take at least three practice swings to every ball hit. Most golfers tend to speed up as they practice, eventually bashing ball after ball without even one practice swing. Any feeling of rhythm and tempo begins to go, the grip gets tighter, and the swing mechanics deteriorate.

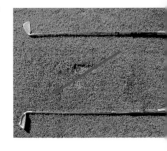

Pause often. Think about what you are trying to accomplish. Feel the clubhead. Hit every club – or at least

Above: Study your divots to see if your swingpath is correct.

Great Golf Tips:

• If your range has sand traps and a chipping and putting green, devote at least half of your time to those areas of the game.

• The most common fault among golfers is swinging too much from out to in, which produces a slice. At the range, work toward developing an inside attack by putting a head cover just outside the ball, or parallel to the target line. Placing another ball about 18 inches (45cm) behind the one you will hit is also useful. The object of both exercises is to force you to bring the clubhead down more inside the target line.

• Try to end the session with a positive strike, even if that means leaving a few balls in the bucket and walking away.

• Many golfers instinctively become competitive at the golf range as they see better players knocking balls far into the distance. As with course play, you should forget others, stay within yourself, and play your own game.

every type of club – in the bag, starting with the wedges and finishing with the driver.

But most importantly, go through the pre-shot routine before every hit. Step back from the ball, pick a specific target, visualize the shot, select an intermediate target to line up with, and take those practice swings. Then set up to the ball with the correct fundamentals in place – just as you would on the course, remembering what Gary Player once said: 'The harder I practice, the luckier I get.'

Playing from the Rough

DURING ANY round, even the best golfers will find themselves in the rough, either along the fairway, deep in the woods, or near the green. Such accidents need not develop from a drama to a crisis, unless the golfer is too ambitious. The rule of thumb? Assess the lie, then get out of jail fast.

Above: Modern utility woods are handy from the semi-rough.

Left: The first rule of thumb in the rough: get out at the first attempt.

Landing in the rough can even be a blessing. Hitting out of long grass can add yards to a well-struck shot – which is known as a 'flyer.' When grass slips between the clubhead and ball, it makes the blade slick and the ball will skid off the face with little or no backspin. But the golfer must know what club to hit, and how to shape his or her shot, which only comes through practice and experience.

This is the time for sober judgement and execution, not heroics. Examine how much grass lies *behind* the ball. If it is only a few blades, then a fairly normal shot may be possible. But if you cannot see the back of the ball, it is time to accept your fate and scale down your ambitions. That might necessitate hitting the ball only a few feet to get onto the fairway, or hitting out sideways, or even backward. But the consolation is that your next shot will be from a good lie, increasing the chances of saving your scorecard from ruin.

For particularly difficult lies, use a sand wedge down to a 7-iron because you need a club that can lift the ball out. The heavy blade of a wedge, and the loft of the shorter clubs, also cut through the grass and debris. This is important because you must hit decisively *through* the ball. Quitting on this shot will leave the ball in a worse position, or even lost.

Play the ball further back in your stance to promote a steeper attack and to avoid contacting too much grass or debris before hitting the ball. Keep your hands forward, and let your weight favor the left side. In addition, open the clubface slightly to avoid getting the club snagged, which will close down the blade and fail to get the ball up and out.

Finally, pick a reasonable target. You do not want to hit back into further rough, or find a hazard around the green. The rough is meant to penalize bad shots and punish golfers who do not respect their limits.

Great Golf Tips:
• If the grass is long and lies against you, take your punishment and use a sand wedge to simply get out. But if the grass is lying toward the target, you have more latitude in selecting a shot.
• In greenside rough, use a lob wedge or sand iron with the face well open. Hit the shot as you would from a bunker.
• Practice in an empty field, or drop a few balls in the rough if the course is quiet. Try a variety of clubs and shots from tough lies to learn how the ball will react and how far it will fly.

Above: Break your wrists early and grip more firmly than usual, then slice across the ball in order to get it up and out of gnarly stuff.

FAIRWAY AND POT BUNKERS

BOTH FAIRWAY bunkers and pot bunkers – often found exclusively on links courses – present unique, but hardly insurmountable, problems even for the average golfer. As with any bunker, the first order of business is not to panic. A well-struck shot, employing the correct technique, can easily get a golfer back on track.

Fairway bunkers are often large enough to afford several options in club selection. If the lip is far enough away, or very low, almost any club can be used – including a fairway wood – as long as you know that making solid contact is the key to this shot.

Pot bunkers must be approached with more respect, and the golfer must know his true capabilities. First, calculate the height of the front lip, taking into account how high you normally hit a sand or lob wedge. Then assess the lie. If it is anything less than excellent, take your medicine and simply find a way out, even if that means hitting sideways or backward.

If you do end up in a bunker, follow these steps to get out of trouble.

• Pick a sensible target and visualize the shot before getting into the bunker.

• Play the ball slightly back in your stance if you have the option of hitting anything but a wedge, and try to nip it cleanly off the surface. Square the clubface, take a normal swing, and hit through the ball to a full finish.

Great Golf Tips:

• Modern utility woods have soleplates designed to escape trouble. Try a 7-, 9- or even 11-wood when practicing.

• If the ball is plugged, square your stance, close the clubhead slightly, and hit down into the sand just behind the ball, keeping the left wrist firm as you accelerate through the ball to an abbreviated follow-through.

• Respect pot bunkers. Even Jack Nicklaus once took four shots to get out of the Hell Bunker at St. Andrews.

• If you must hit a wedge, and the lip is very high, open the clubface, play the ball off your left foot, and think about keeping the body fairly still and centered.

Practice and experience are essential to hitting shots out of fairway bunkers and pot bunkers. Experiment with several different clubs, taking note of how high and far you can hit the ball with varying degrees of loft. If your natural shot pattern is low, keep that in mind when you land in a bunker. Unless the lip is extremely short, or far away, you may have to use a very lofted club to get out.

In other words, do not alter your swing to get the desired results. Instead, use your normal swing and let the correct club do the job.

Above: Assess the lie and height of the lip to select the correct club.

Below: Use your normal swing from a fairway bunker with a small lip and concentrate on nipping the ball off the sand.

PLAYING OFF DIVOTS

MANY GOLFERS turn negative when they find a well-hit shot in a divot, and so are defeated before they start. The key to hitting this shot is to remain positive, and concentrate on taking another divot.

Use a pitching wedge, or try a short iron, especially on approach shots of under 150 yards (137m), which is where most divots lie. Play the ball back in your stance, put more weight on the left side, set your hands in front of the ball and close the clubface slightly. Using a three-quarter swing, concentrate on hitting down and through the ball, taking a second divot *after* the ball.

On long shots, pick an intermediate target and lay up with a short iron, because you will thin or hit fat with more club. But if you own a utility wood with a V-shaped sole, try the 7 or 9 to escape a divot.

Finally, accept that striking the ball precisely is still difficult. If you are hitting into a green, aim for the center, not the pin.

Great Golf Tips:
• Do not use a sand wedge for shots in divots. The extra bounce on the flange will make you thin the ball.
• Practice taking a divot by placing a tee peg an inch or two in front of the ball. Focus on hitting down and through the peg.
• Practice from divots at the range, especially the hardest shot: where the ball lies at the front of the divot mark.

Below: Hitting with confidence is key when cutting through a divot. Trust your set-up and swing, then hit hard through the ball.

TIGHT LIES AND HARDPAN

TIGHT LIES and hardpan often present a double dilemma. First, they inspire terror, which is self-defeating. Secondly, such lies encourage golfers to try to hit up on the ball, which always produces the opposite effect – a thinned or skulled shot. Once again, the key is confidence. Accept that hitting sharply into a ball sitting on tight, short grass – like that found on links courses – or on hard, packed earth is challenging.

Visualize this shot before you hit it, knowing that the ball will fly on a low trajectory and roll considerably once it lands. Through your set-up, which will be much like that for hitting out of a divot, you will be de-lofting whatever iron you use to hit this shot.

Play the ball back, let your weight favor the left side, set your hands forward, and close the clubface slightly. Concentrate on the back of the ball, since you want to strike that first – before the ground or turf – and hit with a steep, descending blow.

Above: One of golf's worst nightmares, the ball lying on hardpan.

Left and above: Concentrate on keeping your weight on the left side to avoid shifting back in an attempt to scoop the ball up, which will result in a skulled shot.

PLAYING OFF LOOSE LIES

W HEN A MIS-HIT shot lands off the fairway on inland courses, the ball is sometimes left sitting on a loose lie, such as a cushion of leaves or pine needles. On links courses, sand and fluffy beach grass are also problems.

If the debris under the ball is deep, you can shoot a clubhead beneath it and leave the ball in place, much like duffing a bunker shot. Disturbing such an unstable lie as you approach is also a worry, since the ball may move, which will cost you a penalty stroke.

Play the ball back in your stance, shift your weight to the left, and keep your hands in front of the ball. Choking down on the club, hover it over the ball to avoid getting the clubface tangled up or disturbing the lie. This set-up should encourage a steep attack, and help you hit the ball before the ground. Pick the club up sharply to a half or three-quarter backswing, then try to sweep the ball cleanly off the surface.

Great Golf Tips:
• Brush away loose debris, but be sure not to move the ball, as this can incur a penalty.
• Do not quit on this shot. Failure to hit decisively through the ball could result in an even worse lie for the next shot.
• Golfers often underestimate how difficult this shot is. Study your situation carefully before deciding on how to proceed.

Below: Do not stab your club into a loose lie. Sweep the ball away.

PLAYING OFF SLOPING LIES

GOLF COURSES are rarely flat, and in any round a player will encounter lies that put his body at odd angles to the ball. However, a few minor adjustments can make a world of difference between lost strokes and a well-struck shot. In effect, you can level the playing field.

On uphill lies – where the ground rises toward the target – a normal stance would result in burying the club in the hillside. Set up with your weight on the right side and shoulders parallel to the slope. However, this lie encourages a hook, so aim right to compensate.

On downhill lies, set up with your weight forward until your shoulders are once again parallel to the slope. Stay as stable as possible throughout the shot, fighting the tendency to fall forward, or to attempt scooping the ball off the turf to gain height. This lie encourages a slice, so aim left to compensate for that trajectory.

Great Golf Tips:
• Take several practice swings, sweeping the club up or down the slope, to avoid the tendency to stab the club into the ground.
• On uphill lies, take more club because the ball will fly higher with less distance. Do the opposite for downhill lies, since the ball will run farther if struck well.
• Play the ball forward for uphill lies, and back for downhill ones.

Below: Use a club to judge the correct angle of your shoulders when playing off sloping lies.

BALL ABOVE THE FEET

WHEN THE ball comes to rest either above or below the feet, the golfer is often tempted simply to take a quick swipe at it. Step back and take a deep breath instead, then focus on the swing adjustments necessary for taming these difficult lies.

With the ball above the feet, you will stand more erect, and your swing plane will be flatter. In other words, you will swing less up and down, and more around your body. That brings the club more inside the target line and closes the clubhead, which can result in a pronounced hook. So aim right to compensate.

Choke down on the club as well, since the ball is closer to you than it would be on flat ground. Depending on the severity of the slope, you might be forced to grip down as far as the shaft. Swing with an even tempo and conviction, and try not to be too ambitious.

Great Golf Tips:
• Failing to choke down will leave the clubhead stuck in the ground before it even reaches the ball.
• As you take the club away, the tendency is to fall backward. Take some practice swings, concentrating on balance.
• On severe slopes, think 'arms and hands,' focusing on a short, controlled swing to avoid swaying into the slope.

Below: Aim right and trust your swing. Staying balanced and maintaining a smooth rhythm are essential.

BALL BELOW THE FEET

MANY GOLFERS fear this shot as much as any in the game. The key is to maintain your balance throughout the swing to negate the effect of leaning over the ball, and the fear of literally toppling over.

Now you will be standing quite close to the ball, so your swing plane will steepen, or be more up and down. The clubhead will also tend to open, resulting in a nasty slice. So aim left to compensate.

Keep your weight on your heels by pushing your bottom as far back as possible, as if you were about to sit into the slope behind you. This will provide stability and keep you from falling forward. Then take more club, because the ball will travel less distance than normal. The added length will also help you extend to the ball.

When you swing, think about staying down. If you come up during the shot, you will top the ball.

Great Golf Tips:
• Take several practice swings, seeing how much weight transfer you can manage before you lose balance.
• Keep your backswing slow, smooth and relatively short, then sweep the clubhead along the slope.
• Stay positive and resist the impulse to raise your head too early in an anxious attempt to see if the shot was struck well.

Below: Sitting down into the slope will promote better balance and a smooth, firm strike on the ball.

CURING A SLICE OR PULL

THE SLICE, and its nasty sibling the pull, are among the most common errors in golf, and usually stem from the same fault: swinging too much from out to in. When the club is delivered to the ball with an open clubface, the result is a slice. The ball travels left, then veers right, losing distance and usually ending up in the rough. But when the clubhead is closed, the result is a pull, or a ball that flies straight to the left.

Curing a slice or pull involves understanding the mechanics of your swing, and the fundamentals of the set-up. Check your grip, posture, and alignment first, then make sure your ball position is correct.

Finally, focus on your swingpath. Aim more to the right and try to swing from in to out. Remember also to turn the hips first on the downswing, then let the shoulders and arms pull the club down to the ball. You may be throwing your shoulders, or 'coming over the top.'

Great Golf Tips:
• If your divots point left, you are swinging too much from out to in.
• Strengthen your grip until you can see three knuckles on the left hand. Lighten your grip pressure as well.
• Practice hitting from a sidehill lie with the ball above your feet to promote a more rounded swingpath.

Below: Poor posture can result in you restricting the backswing and throwing the club from the top. Keep your chin up to allow the shoulders to turn freely underneath.

CURING A HOOK OR PUSH

HOOKING THE ball is less common among average golfers than the slice. That's the good news. The bad news is that the better you get, the more your tendency will be to hook and push the ball, rather than slice it. Hooking causes the ball to fly right to left with a low trajectory and lots of spin, which invariably means trouble, as the ball seems to seek out the worst rough on the course. A push is when the ball flies dead right.

Hooking and pushing are the result of swinging too much from in to out. Control the problem and you will hit a sweet draw.

Again, start with the set-up. Then focus on the swingpath. Hookers tend to grip too tightly, play the ball too far back in their stance, or aim too far right. Square up your stance, play the ball off your left heel, and loosen your grip, especially the right hand.

Finally, try to swing more out to in, cutting the club across the target line. Concentrate on the same swingpath you would use for a bunker shot, although in practice your swing will not be as exaggerated as that. Make sure, also, that you shift your weight back to the left side first, rather than letting your hands lead the downswing.

> **Great Golf Tips:**
> • If your divots point right, your swing is too much from in to out.
> • Weaken your grip, turning both hands to the left.
> • Practice hitting from a sidehill lie with the ball lower than your feet to promote a steeper swing.

Below: Check alignment and focus on pulling the left arm across the ball to cure hooks. Avoid too much hand action.

CURING THIN AND FAT SHOTS

TOPPING OR thinning the ball is often preceded by an attack of the nerves. You see you have a tight lie, or a hazard up ahead that you must clear. Your hands tighten, your body goes rigid, and then you try to lift or scoop the ball into the air. The inevitable result is a swing that is too steep, and thus does not bottom out enough to ensure good contact with the ball, resulting in a thinned shot, or its ugly counterpart, hitting fat.

If you thin the ball, go back to the basics. Check your grip pressure, ball position, and stance. You may be gripping too tightly, the ball may be too far forward, and your posture and weight distribution may be faulty.

Finally, ignore anyone who says you lifted your head, and that you should keep it down. Worrying about that will only restrict your swing. Instead, raise your chin slightly – you cannot turn the shoulders properly unless the chin is out of the way – and drain any pressure out of your body. Then concentrate on making a smooth, rhythmic swing, trusting the loft of the club to lift the ball into the air.

Great Golf Tip:

• Skying the ball and shanking are two other faults that plague many golfers. If you sky from the tee, try pushing the tee peg lower to avoid shooting the clubface underneath. From the turf, concentrate on a smooth, level swing, avoiding the tendency to lift the ball into the air. If you shank – hitting the ball off the hosel – check posture and alignment first, and relax your grip.

Below: Proof positive that you should not keep your head down, or too still, when taking a swing. Such advice leads to topping the ball.

Many golfers tend to fall back on their right side and leave too much weight there in an effort to hoist the ball into the air. The result is a steep swing that cuts across the top of the ball. Alternatively, some golfers dip their left shoulder in an effort to stay in contact with the ball – which can also lead to fat shots – then try to correct that by lifting up through impact and slicing over the top.

Hitting the ball fat is equally destructive and embarrassing. When the clubhead strikes well behind the ball – gouging out a huge divot – the ball usually only rolls a few feet forward before coming to an abrupt stop.

As with a thinned shot, check your grip and ball position and try to distribute your weight evenly between your left and right feet. Hitting fat is often the result of a steep swing, as you try to chop the ball off the turf. Think about making a smooth, level shoulder turn, then taking a slow, deliberate swing, with the clubhead sweeping along the ground at impact to a full follow-through.

Above: Improving your swingpath is the best way to avoid hitting thin or fat shots.

Great Golf Tips:
• Put a tee peg in the ground and aim to sweep it away with an easy, three-quarter swing, concentrating on flattening out the swing arc through impact.
• Check the ball position in relation to your chin. If the ball is too far back in your stance, and your chin is pointed at the ball, you're going to slam the club into the ground and hit fat.

HITTING A DRAW

JACK NICKLAUS once said that the only way to play golf at a high level was to learn how to work the ball both from right to left, or left to right. In other words, if the average golfer wants to improve significantly, he or she must learn how to hit both a draw and a fade. Golf holes are rarely straight, and often demand that you shape shots around doglegs, slopes, trees, water, and sandtraps.

The draw, or modified hook, is a shot that moves the ball from right to left, flies low, and rolls considerably upon landing, which adds distance. It is also a handy shot to possess when coping with the wind.

Start by closing your stance, aiming the feet and shoulders a few degrees to the right. Then close the clubface slightly, so that when you take your grip and stance, it will be square to the target. Finally, swing along the line you have established with your stance, so the club travels from inside the target line to outside.

Great Golf Tips:
• Visualization is a key to hitting the draw. During the pre-shot routine, imagine the ball bending right to left in flight, then rolling to your target.
• Strengthen your grip to promote a swingpath that cuts more inside the target line and delivers a closed clubhead to the ball.
• Focus on trying to roll the hands through impact, with the right crossing over the left.

Below: A closed stance should encourage a flatter swing plane. Try to visualize this as you swing.

HITTING A FADE

OST GOLFERS naturally hit the fade, or more accurately, slice the ball. Learning how to tame and control an outside-to-in swingpath, in order to produce a high-flying, soft-landing shot that moves from left to right, will increase options off the tee and give you a shot to count on when hitting into the green.

Do not worry too much about the loss of distance, either. The gain in control that a fade provides will more than make up for that.

To hit a fade, open your stance slightly, or aim left, and move the ball forward in your stance, placing it just off the left heel. Use a neutral or weak grip, open the clubface slightly, then set it square to the target line. Swing along the line of your stance, cutting across the ball.

Great Golf Tips:

• Weaken your grip slightly by moving both hands to the left, concentrating on the last three fingers of the left hand, which should be firm, while the wrists remain soft.

• Visualize the bending path of the ball in flight and pick a spot where you want it to land before taking your stance. This is a 'feel' shot and you want first to see it in your mind.

• Find some tapes of Lee Trevino and watch him hit the fade. Few golfers before or since have been such masters of this shot.

Left: When hitting a fade, think in terms of more control being exercised by the left side, with the left hand leading the clubface through the ball.

THE BUMP AND RUN

I T IS DIFFICULT to imagine anyone winning the Open Championship without knowing how to hit the 'bump and run.' This nifty little shot is ideal for cheating the wind and hitting into greens with few hazards in the way. But the bump and run is also a handy shot on almost any course.

Set up with your weight favoring the left side and your hands slightly ahead of the ball. Open your stance with the feet and hips pointing left, but your shoulders square. This will encourage a slight in-to-out swingpath and help get the ball rolling. Finally, position the ball in the center of your stance or even slightly behind center.

The swing motion? Try to match the backswing with the follow-through, and keep any body movement to a minimum. A smooth, even tempo is key, while fighting any tendency to decelerate through the ball, which should be almost squeezed off the turf.

Practice and imagination are vital to learning how to hit the bump and run from various distances, so that once on the course, you can visualize the proper shot.

Right: Keep the hands ahead of the clubface when playing the bump and run.

Great Golf Tips:

• Practice the bump and run with a variety of clubs, from a wedge to a 6-iron, and from various distances from 60 to 160 yards (55 to146m).

• Choke down on the club for better feel and control.

• Restrict your follow-through and try to keep your left wrist firm, though never rigid.

THE LOB SHOT

THE SIGHT of a perfectly hit lob shot soaring into the air, then landing softly on the green, is one of the prettiest in golf. But, like most things of beauty, the golfer must appreciate how delicate and rare a good lob shot truly is, and approach hitting one with real respect.

A lob shot is ideal for getting over a bunker, a stream, or any other obstacle to a tight pin placement. But a mis-hit is equally costly, often resulting in you skulling the ball over the green, or a pitiful little stab that leaves the ball plugged in sand or submerged in water.

Set up to the ball with an open stance, pointing your feet, hips and shoulders at least 15 to 20 degrees to the left. Weaken your grip so that the V's point to your chin, then open the clubface of your wedge.

The ball should be positioned off your left heel, with your weight favoring that side. Swing along the line of your stance, breaking your wrists early and sliding the clubhead under and across the ball.

Right: Practice the lob with just the left arm, concentrating on slicing across the ball and finishing with the back of your left hand pointing at the sky.

Great Golf Tips:
• Conviction is key to this shot. Although the pace must be slow and rhythmic, any tendency to decelerate will sabotage the shot.
• Never hit this shot off anything but an ideal lie, where the ball is sitting up on a soft cushion of grass.

SHAPING SHOTS

URING ANY round, a golfer may end up in what appears to be an impossible situation, such as finding his or her ball lying under a towering tree that blocks access to the green. Usually, this means taking one's medicine and punching the ball out sideways. But, sometimes, there are more creative ways of dealing with such obstacles.

Going under a tree or low branches can be accomplished with a version of the bump and run. Use a club with little loft, such as a 5-iron, play the ball back in your stance and close the clubface slightly. Then hit hard, using little wrist action and a low follow-through. The ball will streak out on a low trajectory and travel much farther than you might think.

Going over a tree demands the opposite approach. Use as lofted a club as you can to make the distance needed – if possible – and play the ball forward. With an open stance, keep your hands even with the ball and try to swing across as you would for a fade. But don't try to lift the ball into the air. Trust the club and your swing to do the job.

What if the ball is too close to the tree even to take a

Above: Visualizing these shots before you play them is essential.

Below: Try to take only a three-quarter swing when hooking a shot from right to left around a tree. The spin will make up for lost distance.

stance? Try hitting it left-handed. Turn your club around, so the toe points down. Then reverse your hands on the grip, with the left below the right. This will feel strange, so take several practice swings, limiting your movement to half swings. Finally, take your real swing, keeping it as short and sweet as possible.

What about going right or left *around* the tree? If you have learned to hook or cut the ball, these are the shots to employ, with a few added modifications. The first is to take your stance aiming well right or left of the target, while your clubhead is aimed at the target. Then make a smooth, confident swing, picturing in your mind how the ball will bend around the obstacle in front of you.

Great Golf Tips:

• When trying to hit the ball low under a tree, think of your swing as an exaggerated putting motion. This will help take your body out of the equation and keep the swing movement short and sharp.

• When hitting the left-hand shot, remember that your right arm is the one that leads and should remain extended through impact.

• Bending the ball around a tree calls for a more exaggerated motion than normal, but that shouldn't translate into your swing. Aim farther left or right than you normally would for a shot of this type, but swing with as even a rhythm and tempo as you can muster.

PLAYING IN WIND AND RAIN

Above: Grip down the club for more feel and control on approach shots, and use the bump and run whenever you can.

T HE FIRST and most important rule of thumb when playing in the wind and/or rain is not to let the conditions get the better of you. Just the sight of the wind howling through the trees, or the clouds opening up, often deflates many golfers. The key is to accept that you might not score as well as normal, and then set about meeting the challenge.

Some golfers even enjoy playing in bad weather, especially if they have played or practiced in such conditions before. That gives them something to fall back on, and it might even prove an edge in a competitive match, since other golfers may not have the same experience or the ability to adjust their attitude or game.

Stay focused, work on an even rhythm and tempo, and make careful club selections. Common tendencies, such as swinging harder in the wind, or gripping more tightly in the rain, will simply result in poor shots and lead to frustration.

Constantly read the trees, the flag, or the flight of your playing partners' shots to assess the effect of the wind. Note also how the ball runs in the wind or rain and how the greens are playing.

Right: Shape your shots into a crosswind. Trying to fight the elements will only damage your score, while finding creative ways to cope with them might save your par.

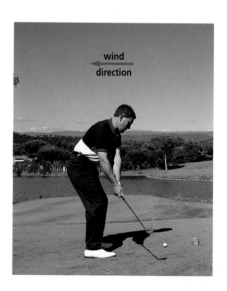

wind
direction

Great Golf Tips:

• Clean your ball when possible, keep mud and debris off your clubface, and tidy up your spikes to ensure you will not slip.

• In a tailwind, use a 3-wood off the tee rather than the driver. The extra loft will get the ball higher into the air, where the wind will help to carry it as far as your driver would normally fly.

• In crosswinds, try to shape your shot so the wind helps the flight of the ball. In a left-to-right wind, aim left along an imaginary target line, allowing the wind to blow the ball to the real target. But do not overdo it. Wind exaggerates spin. A natural fade could turn into an ugly slice.

Above: Study the tops of the trees to gauge the wind direction, even if you do not feel much breeze at ground level.

Great Golf Tips:

• Take more club when hitting into a headwind and accept that you will achieve less distance. Roughly speaking, for every mile per hour of wind, assume you will lose or gain a yard of distance.

• If you can draw the ball, or hit long irons well, do so to produce a low, penetrating flight on the ball, keeping it under the wind.

• In wet weather, the obvious key to an enjoyable round is to keep dry! Carry an umbrella and towel in your bag, and have a set of waterproofs stashed away inside. Hang the towel from the inside of the umbrella and use it to frequently wipe your hands and grips.

THE RULES OF GOLF

KNOWING THE complex rules of golf can avert embarrassment and possible elimination in formal club competition. But beyond that, a thorough understanding of the 'good book' can also help save a golfer strokes. In addition, every golf course has a set of 'local rules' which are printed on the back of scorecards and/or posted in the clubhouse.

In the United States, the rules of golf are administered and interpreted by the United States Golf Association (USGA). *The Rules of Golf*, a small booklet published each year by the USGA is available at most golf clubs for no charge. Get a copy and carry it during a round because it is the responsibility of each player to know the rules, and to live by them.

Except in informal play, a golfer cannot waive a rule, even if his or her playing partners agree to do so. In a

Above: Always carry the official rulebook and know the local rules.

Great Golf Tip:
• If you think your ball is lost off the tee, announce that you are taking a 'provisional.' Hit a second ball, then look for the original. You have five minutes to find the first ball, and if you do, you must play it. If it is lost, however, play the provisional, with a penalty for stroke and distance. You are now hitting your fourth shot.

Left: Check the local rules on your scorecard to see if you are allowed a free drop if your ball lands on a path.

competition, an opponent might challenge such action, and the whole group could be penalized or eliminated from play. Any rule infraction by a player's caddy is also costly, as the player is responsible and therefore will suffer the penalty.

The rules of golf apply equally to amateur hackers and professionals. At the US Masters in 1968, Roberto De Vicenzo signed a scorecard that had the incorrect tally for one hole. That cost him a penalty stroke, and the tournament. In organized competition, always check your scorecard before handing it in.

Knowing local rules can also avert a disaster, and even help scoring. For example, some clubs allow a player to remove debris from a bunker if it interferes with play. But some do not. Rules also vary on how to seek relief – dropping the ball in another place without incurring a penalty – from such obstacles as staked trees, cart paths, sprinkler heads, stakes, and areas of 'ground under repair.'

'Winter rules,' or 'preferred lies,' is another variation. Such rules are temporary and often designated by a sign near the first tee. Invoked during bad weather, these rules are meant to protect the course from further damage and promote fairness. Under winter rules, you can lift and clean the ball – after marking its original location with a tee peg – then place it back on the ground within six inches (15cm), though no nearer the hole. In effect, you can improve your lie and remove anything that might affect the flight of the ball, though your opponents also have the same advantage.

Great Golf Tips:
• If the ball lands in casual water, or you must stand in it to play, you can seek relief. Drop within one club length, but no nearer the hole.
• Do not ask for, or offer opponents advice on yardage or what club to use. Doing so will cost you a penalty stroke.
• You can tap down spike marks only after you have putted. But you can fix pitch marks at any time.

Below: Drop the ball correctly: with your arm outstretched, or at right angles to the body, drop it from shoulder height.

The Etiquette of Golf

GOLF IS one of the few major sports where a participant is not only expected to know how to act, but is required to act accordingly. Failure to behave like a lady or gentleman on the course can be both embarrassing and could be costly to one's score or standing in a club.

But the worst fallout from a lack of etiquette is the modern curse of slow play. A round of golf should not take more than four hours to complete, and can certainly be played on most courses in a time closer to three hours. However, with the popularity of the game increasing, more and more players are now clogging courses, and failing to observe proper golf etiquette.

Great Golf Tips:
• Complimenting your opponent on a good shot or putt is always encouraged in golf etiquette, even if either will beat you.
• Never leave your bag in front of the green. Instead, walk it to an exit point from the green that leads you to the next tee.

Below: Marking your scorecard while you are still on the green holds up play for the group behind you. Do it as you walk to the next tee.

Above: Always rake the sand in a bunker after taking your shot.

Left: You are allowed five minutes to search for a lost ball, but unless you are certain you can find it quickly, avoid slow play by allowing the group behind to play through.

Open the USGA's booklet *The Rules of Golf* – which is free and widely available – and you will see that proper etiquette is both explained and enshrined as a fundamental aspect of the game. Observing etiquette not only speeds up play – which keeps you in a proper rhythm to play well – but also helps avoid situations that can damage your score.

For example, failure to rake a bunker, fix a pitch mark on the green, or replace a divot on the fairway can mean someone else – and next time it could be you – landing in a spot that costs the player at least one stroke or more. Other breaches of etiquette, such as idle chatter on the tee or green, or strolling about while others are playing, can break a golfer's concentration and lead to an errant shot.

One of the worst breaches of etiquette – although sadly all too common – is hitting when another group is still within range. These days, because of slow play, many golfers become frustrated and hit far too soon. The obvious result of this could be a serious injury.

Great Golf Tips:

• Avoid distracting another golfer when he or she is addressing the ball. Stand either behind the person or directly opposite them.

• Two-ball matches have preference and should be allowed to play through. A single player has no 'standing' on the course.

• If a group falls more than one hole behind the players in front, they should immediately let others pass.

• Avoid any damage to the tee or course when taking practice swings, and limit their number. Similarly, be careful that your bag does not scrape the turf, and that the flagstick does not damage the green.

STRATEGY AND SCORING

G OLF IS a game that demands rigorous mental application, as well as physical ability. As Bobby Jones once said, the golfer's true opponent is the course, not other golfers. Professionals always think their way around golf holes. Such an approach is even more vital for the average golfer, who does not have the arsenal of shots that the pros possess. At the end of the day, what really matters are the decisions you make, and the score you record. Style points definitely do not count.

Practice and experience are key elements to course management and scoring. Add a little local knowledge to the mix and you have a real recipe for success. But even a beginner, or a mediocre ball striker, can have an advantage if he or she thinks smart before hitting.

Below left: Find the best line and target off the tee that is consistent with your skill and ability to shape shots.

Below: Avoid trouble by aiming for the heart of the green on most approach shots.

First, know exactly how far you can reasonably hit a ball with any particular club, and off any particular lie. Secondly, apply this knowledge to play within your own capabilities. Thirdly, stay within that comfort level. This will inevitably lead to lower scores.

For example, unless you are a low handicapper, you probably do not have the distance to play long par 4's in regulation. Play the hole as though it were a par 5. Use less club off the tee to avoid trouble, then hit your second shot to within an easy wedge to the green. If all goes right, you will still have a putt for par, and a bogie at worst.

There is nothing wrong with playing bogie golf. If you average a bogie for each hole, just one par will put you into the 80's. Get hot with the putter and you are threatening the 70's. But if you over-reach and go for the low percentage shot, you will quickly run up 6's, 7's, and worse. Now you are struggling to break 100.

Never bring a swing change or the latest tip with you to the course. Save both for the range. Cluttering your mind with technique invariably leads to trouble. Trust your swing and focus on only one key, such as feeling the clubhead, or working on a smooth rhythm and tempo.

But forget even that between shots. Take a deep breath and relax as you walk. Chat with your playing partners, take in the scenery, and try to smell the roses. Remember, golf is a game, and it is supposed to be fun.

GET FIT FOR GOLF

THE UNKIND image of the typical golfer as a flabby weekend warrior is rapidly being put to rest by such superbly conditioned modern pros as Sergio Garcia and Tiger Woods. But in his heyday, Nick Faldo was judged to be as fit as an Olympic athlete. Even the diminutive Gary Player was working out long before it became fashionable, and could sometimes hit drives close to 300 yards (274m) back in the early 1960's.

Forget about buying that new driver or space-age golf ball to improve your game immediately. Instead, start thinking about an exercise regimen that will build strength, plus add flexibility and stamina. Stretching, lifting a few weights, and doing some aerobic exercise will help you both to hit the ball further and improve your short game.

In short, you will play better, feel and look better overall, and avoid possible injury. Strength and flexibility add length to your shots. But getting fitter also adds touch, feel, and control around the green.

Great Golf Tips:

• Before starting an exercise program, talk to your doctor. He or she may recommend a stress test, and can provide guidelines on maximum heart rates for aerobic training.

• Ask a fitness trainer or golf pro to design a regimen for you.

• Keep your neck and knees flexed when exercising, and never put undue stress on your back. Watch the shoulders as well.

• Stretch and warm up for at least ten to 30 minutes before lifting weights or doing any exercise involving major muscle groups.

Below: Always stretch before doing more vigorous exercise, and before and during a round of golf.